Mr. Shipman's Kindergarten Chronicles:
THE FIRST DAY OF SCHOOL
by Dr. Terance Shipman

TEAM SHIPMAN

illustrated by Milan Ristić

ii

Forward

The first day of school is an universal experience. Most people across the country and the world have felt the excitement of the first day of school. I asked my mother, Cloutil S. Davis, if she remembered her first day of school. She told me that she did, and that her older sister had to register and take her to school because my grandmother had to work. My mother said, "I was excited about going to school. I was very eager to learn."

I also remember my daughter's first day of school. It was the only time in my teaching career that I missed a first day of school and missed the excitement of greeting my kindergarten students, but I had to go see my own little girl's first day of school. She cried that day, and I think I did too. I still have the Polaroid picture from that day.

The first day of school is a very important and special day for all students. I hope this book brings back memories that parents and grandparents can share with their children. I hope the book builds energy and eagerness for little ones who are approaching their first day, and I hope the book serves as a guide for new teachers as they prepare for their first day with students. But mostly, I want readers and picture-lookers to just enjoy this book; it's a new classic.

Sincerely,

Terance Shipman, Ed.D.

"And though your beginning was small, your latter days will be very great."

Job 8:7 ESV

Teryn Denae Shipman

Dedication

This book is dedicated to Mrs. Hazel Herring Williams Alexander, a veteran teacher who celebrated over 30 first days of school! As a teacher, Mrs. Williams touched the lives of hundreds, if not thousands of students, and the memory of her class and her instruction brings smiles to those students' faces even today. Teaching in the states of Florida and Georgia, Mrs. Williams was a mentor, teacher, and an inspiration for many students. This book, like Mrs. Williams, exemplifies what good teaching is and the value of a good teacher.

Hazel Herring Williams Alexander

1940 – 2017

"And God hath set some in the church, first apostles, secondly prophets, thirdly teachers, after that miracles, then gifts of healings, helps, governments, diversities of tongues."

1 Corinthians 12:28

"Little brother, I think you are ready for school!" Banicia said to her younger brother, Dewayne, as she came into the living room lugging bags full of school supplies.

Dewayne smiled and sat down on the floor next to his sister and started peeping into the bags. "I got crayons, pencils, a pencil sharpener, a pencil case, and a book bag with my favorite superhero on it!" he bubbled, filled with excitement, "I can't wait to meet my new teacher!"

"Kindergarten is a big year, Dewayne! I know you'll do great!"
Banicia encouraged, and she wrapped her arm around his shoulder,
giving him a hug. "Hey mom," she yelled towards the kitchen, "who's
his teacher anyways?"

Their mom entered the room, smiling at her kids, "Now you know it's Mr. Shipman. I told them I wanted no one else but him! He taught you and your sister, Bricola. There was no way I was letting anyone else be his kindergarten teacher," she said to her daughter, with her hands on her hips and her face set with serious happiness. Dewayne's little head lifted from the notebooks he'd been checking out, and he turned to his sister and asked, "Who's Mr. Shipman?"

Banicia crossed her legs and smiled, "He was my kindergarten teacher. He is my all-time favorite teacher! And now you get to have him!" Their mother sat down on the sofa, and Dewayne moved to sit on her lap and let her help him put paper in his new blue notebook with a dragon on the front. "Banicia," he said, his voice filled with wonder and curiosity, "How's kindergarten? What will we learn? What do you do? Is Mr. Shipman mean?"

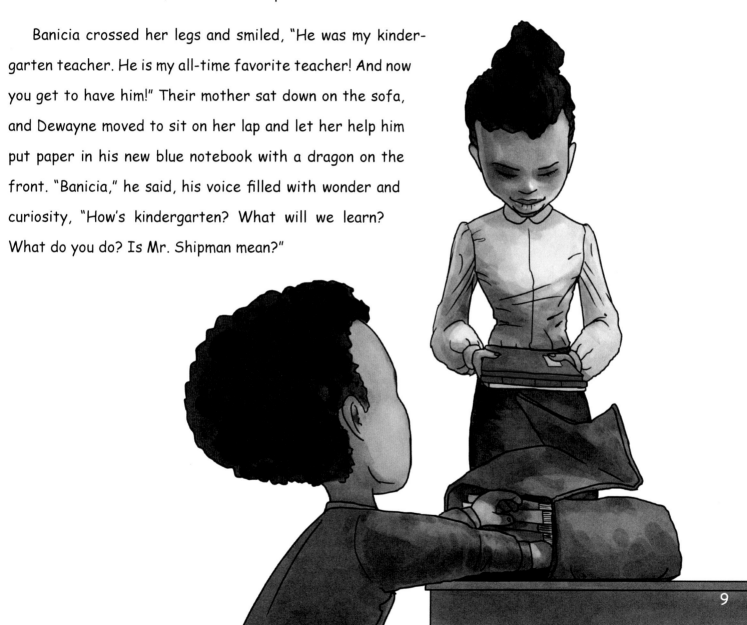

Banicia looked at their mom who chuckled at Dewayne's shaky voice and wide eyes. She knew her little brother was scared, and she decided to tell him about how great her first day of school was in Mr. Shipman's class.

Moving to the sofa with her mom and Dewayne, Banicia began to reflect on her first day of kindergarten. "On my first day of kindergarten," Banicia sang, " I was so excited about going to school."

Mama and I walked down this long hallway.
I had on new shoes and a new jean skirt. Mama
had my hair in my favorite style, and I held her
hand as we walked. There were parents and kids
everywhere.

When we finally got to Mr. Shipman's room, there was a crowd of people around him. All these parents and kids trying to meet him. Some of them were crying, parents and their kids. Some were laughing and taking pictures. But, all of us were excited about being there. The outside of Mr. Shipman's classroom had red, white, and blue colors like the Fourth of July.

Find Out How Great You Can Be

Dewayne listened closely, absorbing every word his sister said. "Mr. Shipman was this tall, young, Black man with this big mustache," Banicia smiled as she continued; "He was smiling at everyone. I watched him while we waited in line. He smiled at everyone and knelt down to the kids. Some of the parents knew him because he'd taught their older kids. But for others, you could tell it was their first time".

Snuggling in his mom's arms, Dewayne whispered, "How could you tell it was their first time, Banicia?" "Well," she continued, "you could just tell." The parents who'd done it before shook Mr.Shipman's hand and said goodbye to their kids. But the new parents, they just didn't leave. They acted like they didn't know how to leave. She shrugged her shoulders and kept telling her story. This one little girl's daddy dropped her off, and she went inside. But as soon as she left and went in the classroom, the daddy began to cry and then he told Mr. Shipman to take care of his baby girl. Mr. Shipman looked at him real serious like, shook his hand and said, 'I will'." She shook her head quite sure she didn't understand parents.

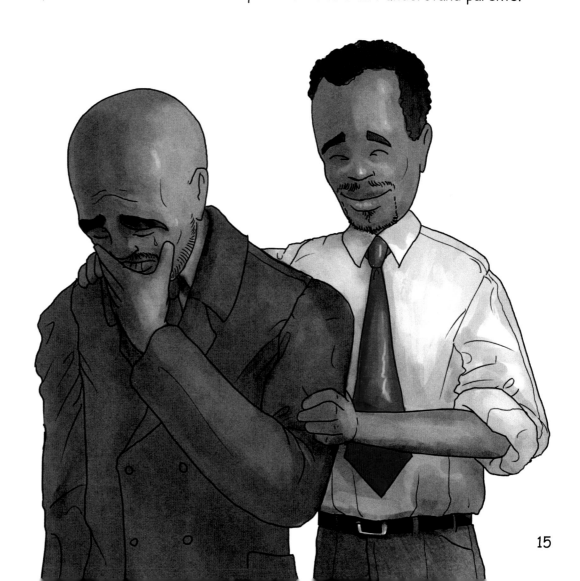

Then it was my turn to meet him. Mr. Shipman knelt down in front of me, smiled and said, "Good morning Sunshine! What's your name?" Their mother interrupted Banicia, laughing about that first day in Mr. Shipman's class. "Banicia was holding on to my leg and acted like she didn't know how to talk, so I gave her a little nudge, and told her to go on and speak to Mr. Shipman."

Banicia sighed, "Mama, let me tell it! I said, 'My name is Banicia', and I shook his hand, looked at him and just like that, I wasn't scared no more!" He had the nicest eyes and smile, and I got a feeling that it was gonna be a great year."

She smiled and picked up Dewayne's pencil box, pencils and helped him put the freshly sharpened pencils in the bright red box with the crayons and glue. "Mr. Shipman was the greatest," Banicia continued, "Welcome to kindergarten", he said. I was ready! I hugged mama, waved bye, and went into the classroom.

When I went in, I looked around, and I knew I was gonna like kindergarten. There was music playing. The room was full of colors, different pictures, shapes, and numbers covered the walls. A ship was hanging from the ceiling and there were colorful rugs on the floor.

Dewayne closed his eyes and imagined a huge pirate ship with real pirates hanging from the ceiling. He didn't know if he liked that or not, so he opened his eyes and looked up at his mom and sister. They didn't seem scared at all. They were smiling and watching him.

"So, what did you do after you looked around?", he asked, still not sold on this whole kindergarten thing, considering that now there may be pirates.

"I saw the little girl whose daddy had cried, and she was crying too. So, I walked over to her, sat down and asked her name. She said her name was Shuree."

"Your friend Shuree who comes over to listen to music with you?" Dewayne gasped excitedly.

"Yeah, that Shuree!" Banicia giggled, "We've known each other since then! You'll make a lot of friends in kindergarten, and some you'll know a long time! But anyway, let me finish the story."

She tickled his feet and continued, I looked at Shuree and she was just crying and crying, and I said "Shuree stop crying, we will be alright! Mr. Shipman's a nice man and he told your daddy he'd take care of you!" Shuree looked up at me, I smiled and told her my name. She stopped crying, and we've been friends since that day!

Excited once again, Dewayne turned to his mom smiling and curious, "Mama, do you think I'll meet a new friend in Mr. Shipman's room?"

His mom tilted her head like she always did and kissed his cheek, replying, "I bet you'll make two or three new friends!"

Banicia nodded and carried on, "Well, there was this lady in the room. She was nice with pretty brown skin and sweet eyes. I didn't know who she was, but she walked right up to me and Shuree and gave us some paper and crayons. I already had crayons in my book bag, but I took hers cause I didn't know what else to do."

"Well hello", she said, "and what are your names?", she asked. I looked at Shuree, she looked at me, and we told her our names. "Well Shuree and Banicia, I'm Mrs. Andrews; I'll be working in here with Mr. Shipman and with you! Can you young ladies draw a picture of yourselves? We would like a picture of your first day of kindergarten." We both nodded our heads, and I began to color a picture of myself in my red shirt with my new book bag.

"Do you think she'll be in my class too?" Dewayne pondered, "What's her name again?"

"Mrs. Andrews," Banicia repeated, "and I'm sure she'll be there! You'll like her too!" But back to the story! There were still kids coming in the room. Some of the parents came in with them. I peeped out the classroom door and saw one little boy. He was blond with big brown eyes, and he was crying harder than Shuree had been. I watched him, his mom and Mr. Shipman. I could tell his mom didn't want to let him go. She was scared.

"Must have been her first time!" Dewayne blurted out. "Well, maybe; but either way, they both were crying really hard, and it wasn't even their turn in line yet." Finally, Mrs. Andrews went over and talked softly to the mom. She looked at Mrs. Andrews, at Mr. Shipman and then at her son and finally let Mrs. Andrews lead them into the classroom. They didn't even speak to Mr. Shipman. I thought that was a little weird. "Sounds a little rude to me," Mama added, looking like she didn't like that part of the story.

"Yeah, well maybe, but I don't know." The boy and his mom came in, and she sat at a table with him, but they both still kept crying.

23

Banicia shook her head and continued, "Mr. Ship-man finally came in the room just as the morning an-nouncements came on."

"What are moaning nownsments?" Dewayne questioned, caus-ing his mother and sister to laugh.

"Not 'moaning nownsments, morning an-nounce-ments." Banicia said slowly, "It's when the principal talks to the whole school on the speaker in the morning. They do it every morning."

"Ohhhh" Dewayne said jumping down off the sofa and grabbing his book bag. Banicia grinned at her little brother and went on with the story of the first day of kindergarten in Mr. Shipman's room. Mr. Shipman asked the parents to say good bye to their children, and Mrs. Andrews had to hold Clifford, the little boy who was crying with his mom. She just rocked him and told him he'd be okay. I was really proud of myself then, because I didn't cry when mama left!

"That's right, baby! You didn't cry and neither did your sister!" Mom said and then she nodded at Dewayne, "And you won't either, big guy! You're gonna do just fine!"

"I know I will!" Dewayne boasted, puffing up his little chest and whipping his book bag trying it on for size.

"Well, Clifford cried!" Banicia stated, "He and his mom!" Then when she left, he stopped. He still sat on Mrs. Andrews' lap, but he wasn't crying anymore. Mr. Shipman had us stand for the Pledge of Allegiance. We had no idea what that was, but we did it. After we sat down, Mr. Shipman was still standing.

Banicia stood imitating Mr. Shipman, "GOOD MORNING CLASS," she bellowed, "and he was smiling the whole time! And we smiled back at him." Shuree giggled, and even Clifford started to smile. She strolled back and forth in front of the sofa across the living room, stretching herself tall and smiling, trying to move and speak like Mr. Shipman had when she was in his kindergarten class.

"I woke up this morning and I asked myself, Mr. Shipman! Is today going to be a good day or bad day?" She held her arms wide and continued to mimic her teacher, booming with glee, "A GOOD DAY!" Then this kid named Cameron jumped up all excited and happy, and yelled, "YES! It's gonna be a good day!" Mr. Shipman smiled but he didn't stop, "Class repeat after me: Today will be a GOOD DAY! Point to somebody and say, today you will have a marvelous day!"

She strutted towards Dewayne, doing her best imitation of her favorite teacher and leaned forward smiling brightly and cheered. "Point to somebody else and say, today you will have fantastic day! Now give yourselves a hand!" She began to clap and so did Dewayne, as he became more and more excited about the first day of kindergarten in Mr. Shipman's class.

Clifford was still sitting in Mrs. Andrews' Lap, but he was smiling. And parents were still standing at the door peeping in and most of them were smiling. Me and Shuree were laughing and holding hands! We just knew it was gonna be a good day! The principal came on again and announced that it was time for all the parents to leave the building. And even though Clifford wasn't even crying, his mom was the last to leave. She wasn't smiling, but she did finally go."

Well, maybe for a minute, then he noticed she was going to leave and started crying for her again. We all covered our ears, but Mrs. Andrews had him calmed down in no time. She was really good at that! In no time, he was grinning again and enjoying his first day of kindergarten in Mr. Shipman's room. But he did keep on saying he wanted his mama. "So is that all you do in kindergarten," Dewayne asked.

"Well no silly! That day we did a whole lot more! We had circle time"

"Is that when you practice spinning in circles?" Dwayne giggled, tickling himself with his joke.

"You are silly today," his mom said, pulling him back on the sofa and cuddling him close.

Circle time is when we sit on the floor in a circle and talk to each other, read books, sing, or whatever the teacher tells you to do. On the first day in Mr. Shipman's class, we introduced ourselves during circle time. Mrs. Andrews went first. Clifford wouldn't speak to the class, but we all said good morning to him.

I remember everyone in that class. There was David, Maesa, William, Shuree, Hayden, Joseph, Tatiana, Alyesia, Autumn, Sarafina, Leodrea, Cameron, JaMarcus and, of course, Clifford. I remember Shuree and I were Black and so were, Alyesia, Leodrea, Cameron, Hayden, JaMarcus, and Autumn. Tatiana and Sarafina were multi-cultural, William, Tiffany, Clifford and David were white, Joseph was Asian and Maesa was Hispanic. JaMarcus was taller than everyone and Leodrea was kind of chubby but cute. Shuree looked so little, she was short! We were all different shapes, sizes, and colors. But, we were all kindergarteners and we all were excited!

"I'm gonna be the tallest in my class!" Dewayne proclaimed.

"Well maybe you will be! But don't be like JaMarcus. While we were at circle time, he tried to get up and go play with the toys."

"There are toys!" Dewayne squealed, leaning forward, eyes wide and smiling widely. "Yes! Lots of toys!" I almost got out my seat to play with them too! But don't play with them until Mr. Shipman tells you can or you'll get in trouble like Jamarcus did at circle time. Mr. Shipman had to tell him to come back to the circle. He looked so sad, then Mr. Shipman told him not to be sad cause we'd play with the toys later, but we had to learn to sit and wait.

Dewayne nodded, focusing hard on what his sister was saying. Then after we finished telling everyone our names and saying good morning, Mr. Shipman began to teach us songs to sing. It was fun. Then after we'd sang for a while, we got up and took a restroom break. We saw all the other classes in the hallway. And that was cool cause we realized that we knew a lot of other kids in kindergarten from our neighborhoods and we were all waving at each other, but we couldn't talk cause Mr. Shipman had told us how important it was to be on silent in the hallways.

"Banicia," their mother asked, "was Mrs. Andrews still holding Clifford?"

Banicia sighed and giggled, "No," he'd finally stopped crying and was just holding her hand, but every five minutes he asked, "When do we get to go home?" Mrs. Andrews would hug him, and Mr. Shipman would say "Later today Clifford and smile."

"Poor Clifford," Mom said shaking her head. "You'll enjoy tomorrow, Dewayne, don't you worry about coming home! Just enjoy being in kindergarten!" "I think I will Mom" Dewayne stated with pride.

So, after we went to the bathroom, we went on a building tour which was kind of fun. Mr. Shipman took us to see the principal, Dr. Luck, and the assistant principal, Mrs. Johnson. They were so nice. Dr. Luck said, "Welcome to Tiny Laster Elementary School. I'm so very glad that you are here!" and Mrs. Johnson said, "You have two very good teachers." They smiled at us and then shook our hands.

M. Gla

Then we went into the library. It was in the center of the school. I'd never seen so many books. Mrs. Haywood was the librarian, and she was reading to a class when we came in but when she saw us, she waved and said, "Well Hello, Team Shipman!" Maesa asked Mrs. Andrews, what was Team Shipman. She explained to us that the class, our parents, and Mr. Shipman: we were Team Shipman! Banicia smiled and pumped her fist in the air with pride!

"Will I be on Team Shipman too?" Dewayne asked. "Yep, you sure will! And that, little brother is the place to be when you're in kindergarten!"

We went through the gym and saw the big kids exercising. A tall man came towards us. He wasn't dressed like Mr. Shipman, who had on a suit. This guy had on shorts and a t-shirt that said Laster. He smiled and said, "Well look at the new Team Shipman! Good morning! I'm Coach Benford, your P.E. teacher."

Again, Banicia stood and began to imitate Coach Benford. "I look forward to seeing all of you on tomorrow." She smiled, poked out her stomach and leaned back, like she remembered her old P.E. teacher doing.

Dewayne imagined that Coach Benford was a big guy with a big tummy, "Banicia," he asked, with his big brown eyes soft and relaxed, "what's P.E.?"

"Well, P.E. is a class where you go exercise and play. It's one of the best classes of the day!" After Coach Benford talked to us, he and Mr. Shipman shook hands and we went back to the classroom for story time.

"I love story time! Don't I Mama!" Dewayne gushed! "Yep, you sure do! Every night you want two or three stories!"

Well you'll have story time almost every day in Mr. Shipman's class and he's good at reading too! On the first day, Mr. Shipman read us a book about the color brown. We loved it. In fact, Tatiana said, "I never knew brown could be so beautiful." And Leodrea said, "Yeah, just like me!" We all laughed at them and Mr. Shipman had us color pictures with only the color brown. Mrs. Andrews put our pictures up on the wall. David colored donuts because he said he liked them and Leodrea drew a picture of herself in a beautiful brown dress.

"What did you draw, Banicia?" Dewayne interrupted.

 "I drew us, a picture of Mama, Bricola, and me." "You didn't draw me too?"
Dewayne questioned his sister looking sad cause he'd been left out.

"No, silly, I couldn't draw you, you weren't born yet!"

Dewayne giggled and smiled, "Ohhhh, that makes sense."

   After we finished coloring, we washed our hands and lined up to go to lunch.

We went into the lunchroom and met the lunchroom staff. Mr. Shipman, Mrs. Andrews, and the lunchroom staff helped us get our lunches, and we all sat down and ate a good lunch. Clifford even stopped crying and wanted more to eat. Alyesia needed help opening her milk and Joseph showed her how to do it. Then Mr. Shipman and Mrs. Andrews showed us how to clean up, empty our trays and put them up. "Was it time to go home after you ate?" Dewayne asked.

"No, after lunch we went to the bathroom, washed up, and then it was nap time."

"Ugggggghhhhh!" Dewayne moaned, "I hate nap time."

"But you have to have nap time," Mom said, "so you can grow and be strong."

G. GELLMAN'S CAFETERIA

"Yeah," Banicia agreed, and it wasn't too bad. Mr. Shipman played soft music and turned the lights down low. Some kids had mats and pillows or towels and some just laid their heads down on the table. And besides, that's when Mr. Shipman and Mrs. Andrews ate. Dewayne rolled his eyes and shook his head, "I still don't think I'm gonna like nap time, but I guess I want to grow and be strong, and I guess this Mr. Shipman guy has to eat" he shrugged.

Banicia laughed at her brother, "Boy, you crazy! Yes, they got to eat, and guess what comes after nap time." "What?" Dewayne gasped eagerly.

"Recess!" It's one of the best parts of kindergarten and the whole day! We went outside, and William tried to run for the playground.

But, Mr. Shipman told him no and then said "We do exercises first as a team. Class this is how you do a jumping jack." Banicia got up and did jumping jacks. "I can do that!" yelled Dewayne jumping up and joining his sister as she exercised. "Then he had us doing waybacks" she said, stretching her arms above her head and then arching her back and trying to bend back as far as she could.

Dewayne joined in on that too, and as he bent backwards, he tumbled over causing his mom and sister to chuckle. "A little too far Dewayne," Mom said as he stood up and tired again.

"Good Job," Banicia told him, "now try arm circles and you'll be ready for Mr. Shipman, just as ready as can be!" We did these every day and every day Maesa asked, "Can we go to the playground now Mr. Shipman?" He'd just smile and say, "Spread out and let's get these exercises done" And we'd get into a circle, hold our arms out to make sure our hands didn't touch, and Mr. Shipman would lead us in exercise. It was so much fun and then we went to the playground.

43

"Tell me about the playground" Dewayne asked jumping up and down. "Well there was a slide, monkey bars, the wall climber, the swings, the seesaw, and these little rocking horses. And there was an area with big tires you could climb on and lots of space to run around." We always had fun, and then we had a water break and we cleaned up before going back inside. Mr. Shipman let us drink as much water as we wanted, and Mrs. Andrews always had cool paper towels for us to wipe our faces off.

Banicia sat down and fanned her face. "Being on the playground makes you hot!" Dewayne blurted out.

"Yes, it does," Banicia agreed. "But, when we went back inside, we had center time and that was cool!"

Dr. D.S. BATTLE PLAYGROUND

On the first day, Mr. Shipman told us all about the different centers in the classroom. There was a science center, math center, an art center, a dress up and puppet center, but my favorite center was the reading center. Mr. Shipman would allow two or three of us at each center, then there was the loft center, and only two kids were allowed up there at one time.

"That sounds boring." Dewayne said, thinking he'd just want to stay on the playground all day.

No, the centers are a lot of fun! In the art center, Mrs. Andrews helped us make handprints with paint and over in the puppet center. Autumn and Hayden always did these cool puppet shows for us and made us laugh. And Mr. Shipman had soooo many books in the reading center and he's always adding new ones! "I loved to go to the reading center!"

"It still doesn't sound as fun as the playground." Dewayne pouted.

"Yeah, but don't be like Clifford. He got in trouble for chasing Sarafina around the room and sent to time out for five minutes." Dewayne's older sister gave him a firm look.

He stretched his eyes wide and said, "Oh no! I won't get in trouble like Clifford, I'll do the centers!"

Good!" Banicia said, "Then all you have to do is listen for Mr. Shipman. He'll say, 'Freeze!' and that means it's time to clean up your area and move to a new center, so you got to learn the clean-up song. Do you know it?"

Dewayne thought for a moment, "No I don't know it... teach me."

"Well it's the perfect song to sing right now," Dewayne's mom said, "so you can clean up this room. Look at this mess you made!"

Dewayne looked at the floor, and sure enough, there were bags, and wrappers everywhere. "Okay, the song is easy," Banicia said, "It goes like this: clean up, clean up, everybody clean up, pick it up, put it up, everybody clean up. Now you sing!"

And Dewayne did. Their mom did too. And they all cleaned up the living room.

"Hooray!" Dewayne cheered as they finished cleaning the room.

"See, center time will be fun. After center time is alphabet time! And I know you'll do great then!"

"He sure will!" their mom added, "He already knows his letters, and Mr. Shipman is gonna nail in those sounds!"

"He gonna put nails in me!" Dewayne gasped.

"No boy! But, you will learn the alphabet story. Mr. Shipman read it to us. Then Dewayne said, "I can't wait until tomorrow! I'm so excited!" After the story, Mr. Shipman told us we were going to make a video about the alphabet and their sounds, But, I told him I already knew my A-B-C's! My mama taught them to me at home. And then Mr. Shipman smiled at me proudly and said, 'Well now then Ms. Banicia, you can help me teach the other students.' I was really proud of that and said, 'Okay Mr. Shipman! I will!'"

Banicia smiled, as she remembered how good she felt on her first day of kindergarten in Mr. Shipman's class.

50

"Man, kindergarten sounds like it'll make you tired." Dewayne said trying on his bookbag filled with all his new supplies.

Well, you know you've done something important when you finish that first day. And by the time you finish the Alphabet Story, it'll be time to go home. That's when you get to put on your bookbag again and line up. Mr. Shipman will probably say, 'Today was a good day!' "How do you know what he'll say, Banicia?" Dewayne questioned his sister with a little attitude in his voice.

"Cause that's what he said to us all the time, then he'd say, 'NO! It was a marvelous and fantastic day!' And you know what?" Banicia said, leaning towards her brother smiling.

"What?" Dewayne replied smiling.

It was a marvelous and fantastic day! Even Clifford ended up having a good day, in fact, after we had our book bags on, Clifford walked up to Mr. Shipman and announced, "I think I like you, Mr. Shipman!" and Mr. Shipman knelt down to him and said, "I think I like you too! I like you too," he said pointing at Hayden, "and you and you and you too!" He laughed pointing at several kids around the room. We all laughed and started to tell each other that we liked each other.

Then Mrs. Andrews said, "Well what about me?" We all laughed, ran and gave her hugs. Banicia leaned back and signed "And that was pretty much the end of the day." Mrs. Andrews took the kids who rode buses to the bus ramp, and Mr. Shipman took the kids who got picked up or walked home to the front of the building.

Shuree and I held hands on the way to the car line, but when she saw her dad, she ran to him, he picked her up, kissed her, and they started talking. "Daddy! School was so much fun," she announced and then she said all proud, "I'm a part of Team Shipman!" Her dad laughed, "Well what's Team Shipman?" her dad asked. Shuree looked over at Mr. Shipman who was smiling at her and said, "It's me, Mr. Shipman, Mrs. Andrews, the other kids in my class, the parents and you and mama too!" Her daddy looked surprised, and he walked over to Mr. Shipman and said, "Thank you for today, Mr. Shipman" and shook his hand. Mr. Shipman just gave him a big ole smile and said, "It was my pleasure! Welcome to Team Shipman!"

Then Clifford's mom came running up to him. Everybody just watched to see what Clifford would do. "Did he start crying again?" Dewayne asked.

"No, his mom hugged him, kissed him, and asked him if he was okay." Clifford smiled, "Yeah mama, I'm fine. I like Mr. Shipman, Mrs. Andrews and the other kids!" She seemed surprised and said, "You do!" But Clifford just smiled and said, "Yes, I'm part of Team Shipman! I met Sarafina, Jamarcus, William, Shuree, Hayden and a bunch of other kids!" His mom looked at Mr. Shipman, "Well okay Clifford, let's just go home!" She tried to pick him up and leave, but Clifford pulled away and ran up to Mr. Shipman and said, "Bye Mr. Shipman, I'll see you tomorrow!" and he waved. Mr. Shipman waved and smiled at him.

When he left, I finally saw mama and ran over to her and hugged her. It was good seeing her again. She gave me a card to take to Mr. Shipman, so I ran back and handed it to him and told him good bye.

"Mama, what did the card say?" Dewayne smiled at his mom and leaned on her lap.

I told him thank you for being a teacher. I thanked him for being a positive male role model for all his students!

"Wow!" Dewayne whispered, "You did all that on the first day of school?"

"Yeah, Team Shipman did a lot on the first day of school!" And I hear Mr. Shipman has gotten even better!

"I can't wait for school to start!"

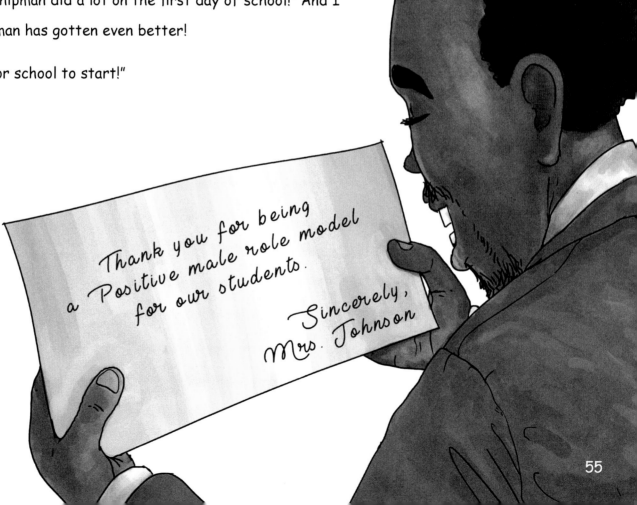

Thank you for being a positive male role model for our students.

Sincerely,
Mrs. Johnson

Dr. Terance Shipman is a 25-year veteran teacher. He spent much of his teaching career working with elementary aged students. In fact, he spent his first 11 years teaching kindergarten! He is proud to say that he has built strong relationships over those years with a supportive network of former students, their parents, and co-workers. Dr. Shipman calls this ever- developing network "Team Shipman". His goal for Team Shipman is to offer continual encouragement, leadership, and mentorship to his students, their families, and his professional peers. Dr. Shipman currently teaches middle school and extends membership to Team Shipman to these students and their families, as well.

Mr. Shipman's Kindergarten Chronicles are the stories of teaching that make Dr. Shipman smile the most when he thinks about his years teaching kindergarten. Each book in the series celebrates the male teacher, in particular the Black male teacher. Acknowledging the underrepresentation of Black men in education, Mr. Shipman is a positive and strong male image that children need. Through his first series of books, Mr. Shipman's Kindergarten Chronicles, Dr. Shipman makes kindergarten an exciting and anticipated adventure for students, parents, and teachers, while casting an even wider net for Team Shipman.

Dr. Shipman received his Bachelor's degree in Elementary Education from the Tuskegee University in 1992. After obtaining this degree, he attended Hampton University in Virginia and obtained a Master's degree in Elementary Education in 1994. For the next 13 years, Dr. Shipman was an elementary teacher in the Atlanta Public School System. Most of his time at APS was spent as a kindergarten teacher, and in 2009 he earned his Educational Specialist degree from the University of West Georgia in Administration Supervision and soon after he complete his doctoral degree at Clark Atlanta University in 2013. Since completing his final degree, Dr. Shipman has worked with middle school and high school aged students. And through it all, Team Shipman is still growing!

How many apples, ships,
and question marks
are hidden in the book?
Go to
www.teranceshipman.com
to find
the answers.

TEAM SHIPMAN

Then and Now

Liked this book?

Check out the first book of the
Mr.Shipman's Kindergarten Chronicles Series!

Get it now!

Available at Amazon, Barnes & Noble, Walmart

and

www.teranceshipman.com

Made in the USA
Las Vegas, NV
02 June 2021